HARRIER
Inside and Out

Mark Attrill

The Crowood Press

First published in 2002 by
The Crowood Press Ltd
Ramsbury, Marlborough
Wiltshire SN8 2HR

British Library Cataloguing-in-Publication Data
A catalogue record for this book is available from the British Library.

ISBN 1 86126 500 X

Photograph previous page: A pair of Harrier GR.7s from 20(R) Sqn
(foreground) and 1(F) Sqn keep station with a two-seat T.10 operational
trainer, also from 20(R) Sqn, high over central England. The aircraft
wear the two-tone overall green colour scheme that was then in vogue.
(Photo: copyright BAe Systems plc)

Typeset by Shane O'Dwyer, 132 William Street, Swindon

Printed and bound in Malaysia by Times Offset (M) Sdn. Bhd.

Contents

Introduction

This book has been put together primarily with the aeronautical engineer, aviation enthusiast or scale-aircraft modeller in mind. It does not attempt to cover the history of the Harrier's design, development or operational service in any amount of detail, since there are countless books on these aspects of this unique aircraft. A brief look at the development of the Harrier family is appropriate since it will help the reader to understand the subtle differences between the early Hawker Siddeley/British Aerospace marks of this aircraft. The text also outlines the significant changes made to the basic design in order to produce the more advanced second-generation British Aerospace/McDonnell Douglas AV-8B Harrier II family, which is currently in service with a number of air arms. It concentrates on those aircraft in service with the Royal Air Force and Fleet Air Arm, although a small number of photographs of Harriers in service with foreign air arms are included, for comparative purposes.

Royal Air Force Harriers

The first-generation Hawker Siddeley Harrier GR.1 was a direct derivative of the earlier P.1127 and Kestrel conceptual aircraft, which had been successfully developed to meet a number of air staff requirements from air forces of Great Britain, the United States and Germany. The P.1127 and Kestrel proved Sir Sydney Camm's design concept for a Vertical or Short Take-Off and Landing (V/STOL) fighter aircraft. By the end of 1965, Hawker Siddeley Aviation Limited had received an order for six development aircraft, known as the P.1127(RAF).

This aircraft, later to be called the Harrier GR.1 in Royal Air Force Service, differed considerably from the original P.1127. It was virtually a new aircraft. The Rolls-Royce Pegasus 6 engine, later known as the Mk 101, and rated at 19,000lb, was at its core. To meet the revised specification of the Pegasus 6, the intakes of the P.1127(RAF) were redesigned, while six (subsequently eight) 'blow-in' auxiliary intakes were added on each side of the air intake. The mainplane was further redesigned with prominent vortex generators, wing fences and tip extensions. The basic geometry of the original P.1127 was retained although the undercarriage underwent a fundamental change, with strengthened legs and a different gear door arrangement, to facilitate the use of operational aircraft from unprepared surfaces or in the field.

Most of the avionics suite from the original P.1127 was retained, although several new systems, including autostabilization, were incorporated. An inertial navigation/attack system, the Ferranti FE541, with a Smiths Head-Up Display (HUD) and moving map display, provided the degree of accuracy in ground attack and navigation capabilities that the Royal Air Force required in this new fighter aircraft. In recognition of its operational role, the aircraft received five weapons/stores pylons on the wings and fuselage centreline. The inner wing stations were plumbed for the carriage of 100- or 330-gallon jettisonable fuel tanks. The aircraft possessed no internal gun armament so provision was made for two 30mm Aden cannon in under-fuselage pods. For the tactical reconnaissance role the aircraft was fitted with a port oblique 70mm camera in the nose, supplemented by a centreline-mounted recce pod, which could house a further five cameras.

The first of the six development batch aircraft came off the Kingston line in 1966 and all were employed in development work, either for the aircraft manufacturer, Rolls-Royce or the Royal Aircraft Establishment at Boscombe Down. The first of 60 Harrier GR.1s, XV738, first flew on 28 December 1967 and it was envisaged that the aircraft would equip the training unit and an operational squadron at RAF Wittering. Wittering had been designated as the main operating base in the UK, with a second frontline squadron based in RAF Germany. The production aircraft differed slightly from the development batch aircraft in having slight larger intakes and eight blow-in doors on each intake side, to cater for the increased thrust of the Pegasus Mk 103 engine, although the first and second batches of GR.1s were built with the Mk 101 engine. With deliveries of the first production aircraft to the Royal Air Force, the Harrier Conversion Unit formed at RAF Wittering in April 1969. Some four months later Number 1(F) Squadron started to work up on the new aircraft.

The Harrier GR.1 eventually equipped a further three frontline squadrons, Nos 3(F), IV(AC) and 20, all at RAF Wildenrath in RAF Germany. Shortly after their complete introduction to RAF service, most of the aircraft received the reworked Pegasus Mk 102 engine and were redesignated GR.1A.

During the same period, the US Marine Corps had completed its evaluation of the new aircraft and had been impressed by the Harrier's ability to fly Close Air Support (CAS) missions from ships or unprepared strips. This particular capability had been explored during the development of the P.1127. The US Government agreed a licence deal between McDonnell Douglas and Hawker Siddeley Aviation in 1969, which saw deliveries of the AV-8 (as the aircraft

A unique formation with no fewer than five variants of the Harrier airborne for a 'family' photocall. *From top to bottom:* a Harrier GR.7 of 1(F) Sqn, a Sea Harrier FRS.1 of 899 Naval Air Squadron, a two-seat Harrier T.4 of 1(F) Sqn, a Harrier GR.3 of 233 OCU and a Harrier GR.5 of 233 OCU. (Photo: copyright BAe Systems plc)

became known in USMC service) between 1970 and 1975. A total of 110 aircraft – comprising 102 single-seat AV-8As and eight two-seat TAV-8As – were finally delivered to the USMC. Externally, the aircraft differed little from the Harrier GR.1 although the uprated Pegasus Mk 103 engine and the carriage of AIM-9 Sidewinder missiles were specified for the US service. The aircraft also possessed a much simpler navigation/attack system since the USMC did not envisage using it for a wide range of roles. Later in its service life the AV-8s also received the Stencel ejection seat, an indigenous product, as part of a broad US plan to standardize the ejection-seat systems on a number of US Navy and USMC aircraft types.

The AV-8 initially equipped three frontline USMC squadrons and a training unit. VMA-231 'Ace of Spades' and VMA-542 'Flying Tigers' operated from MCAS Cherry Point in North Carolina on the east coast. The USMC AV-8 training unit, VMAT-203 'Hawks', which operated all eight of the services' TAV-8As, was also stationed at Cherry Point. The remaining frontline squadron, VMA-513 'Flying Nightmares', was first operated from Cherry Point although in later years it relocated to MCAS Yuma, Arizona. Following acceptance trials at the USMC test facility at Patuxent River, the AV-8 Harrier was cleared to operate from both amphibious assault carriers and the smaller LPDs, which were only equipped with a rear landing platform. As a result, the modus operandi for the AV-8 regularly included deployment aboard the USMC's indigenous helicopter carriers as well as established airfields and dispersed sites. In

1979 the USMC decided to rework its surviving AV-8As in order to retain the aircraft in service until the arrival of the much-heralded second-generation AV-8B Harrier, scheduled for 1985.

A Service Life Extension Programme (SLEP) provided modest improvements to the aircraft's capability, which included new Lift Improvement Devices (LID) and a retractable ventral dam on the fuselage undersurfaces, similar to the system that would eventually be fitted to the AV-8B. Other changes included Radar Warning Receiver (RWR) equipment in the tailcone, ALE-39 chaff/flare dispensers in the rear lower fuselage and the deletion of the oblique F95 camera in the nose. These aircraft, now known as AV-8Cs, continued in service until mid-1986, by which time AV-8B deliveries to the frontline squadrons had been completed.

Two other nations have operated the so-called 'baseline' Harrier AV-8. Spain's Naval Air Arm followed the USMC in operating the AV-8 from aircraft carriers. Due to the British embargo imposed on Spain during the 1970s, the aircraft had to be ordered through the US Navy, which were contracted to supply six AV-8s and two TAV-8s in July 1973. In Spanish Navy service the aircraft were referred to as AV-8A(S) and TAV-8A(S) and gained the unofficial name of 'Matador'. The AV-8S wore a matt gull grey and white colour scheme, not dissimilar to that worn by USN of the period. A further five single-seat AV-8Ss were ordered in 1977. In 1987 the aircraft received a mid-life update and were equipped with Marconi Sky Guardian RWRs. The twin 30mm Aden gun pods were retained and standard offensive weapons mirrored those of the USMC and included iron bombs and 5in Zuni rockets. The Eighth Flight (Esla 8) of Spanish Naval Aviation became the sole operator of the type, forming at Cadiz/Rota in September 1976, and regularly deploying on the Spanish Navy carrier *Dedalo*.

Following the delivery of new AV-8B Harrier IIs to the Spanish Armada, the Royal Thai Navy purchased nine surviving AV-8S and TAV-8S airframes from Spain in 1993. These aircraft are now operated by No 105 Squadron, part of Royal Thai Navy Wing 1, based at U-Tapao.

In spite of an initial requirement for a two-seat version of the P.1127(RAF), this was not followed up until after the introduction to service of the single-seat Harrier GR.1. Production priority had been given to the single-seat variant Harrier but, following the lessons learned from the introduction to service of the English Electric Lightning, the RAF was keen to acquire a two-seat version of the Harrier to aid conversion to a radically different combat aircraft.

As a result, the prototype two-seat variant, to be known as the Harrier T.2, first flew in April 1969. The aircraft was primarily to be used as a conversion trainer but the RAF also wanted the aircraft to have a fully operational capability so the T.2 retained the same nav/attack system, F95 camera nose and stores stations on the wings and fuselage.

The design of a two-seat Harrier variant was no easy feat since changes to the centre of gravity, brought about by the installation of a second cockpit, had to be kept within the bounds imposed by the centre of thrust, particularly with a V/STOL design. The options open to the Hawker Siddeley team at Kingston were limited and, following a number of design proposals, it was decided to extend the nose forward in a tandem seating layout, with changes to the rear fuselage to counter the effects of the longer nose. The tailfin was mounted further back and heightened, to maintain weathercock stability, while a large underfin was also added. The fuselage-mounted reaction control valves were moved in order to maintain their effectiveness. The forward one was moved to near the nose while the rear extremity of the fuselage was much extended to house the rear (pitch and yaw) reaction control valve. A completely new cockpit canopy was designed, which hinged sideways. The rear cockpit, with its own integral windscreen, duplicated virtually all of the instrumentation in the front cockpit with the exception of the moving map display.

The flight testing of the two-seat Harrier was problematic, revealing difficulties with directional stability, brought about by the fin area. As a result the height of the fin was increased incrementally during flight testing and a final standard was not agreed until after the first of the initial batch of twelve T.2s were coming off the production line at Kingston/Dunsfold. As a result, two-seaters were seen in service with varying heights of fins before the complete batch of aircraft were retrofitted with the standard fin. In spite of these early problems the aircraft retained the excellent handling of the GR.1 and possessed a great deal of commonality, in terms of maintenance and support, with the single-seat aircraft. The largest concentration of two-seat aircraft was to be found with Number 233 Operational Conversion Unit at RAF Wittering, although the frontline squadrons each received two or three aircraft as well.

In 1974 the RAF ordered twelve new-build single-seat aircraft as attrition replacements; these aircraft, fitted with the Pegasus Mk 103 engine from the outset, were designated GR.3. The aircraft, delivered during the course of 1976, were equipped with a new suite of avionics, which also provided the most noticeable modification made to the single-seat Harrier since its introduction to service. A Ferranti Laser Ranging and Marked Target Seeker (LRMTS) was fitted in an extended 'Dolphin' nosecone with a Passive Warning Receiver (PWR) fitted to the fin and rear fuselage. The LRMTS was closely aligned to the system fitted to the RAF Jaguar and provided the two ground-attack fighters with a degree of commonality in their combat roles. The primary function of the equipment was to provide more accurate laser pulse derived range information on ground targets and a IR target search capability. The LRMTS, first factory-fitted to the original GR.3 attrition batch, was subsequently retrofitted to all those single-seat Harriers that remained in RAF service by 1979. It made drastic improvements in target acquisition and bomb delivery accuracy, especially in the single-pass lay-down attack mission profile.

The fitting of the Passive Warning Receiver (PWR) system involved the mounting of two antennae to the leading edge of the fin and in the tailcone. The fin surfaces were recontoured and enlarged, both to accommodate the forward-looking PWR and to counter the destabilizing effect of the LRMTS mounted in the new 'Dolphin' nose. As its name suggests, the PWR processed incoming signals from radars illuminating the Harrier as a target and presented the pilot with a range of information from which he could decide what avoiding action to take in the face of a possible attack. When the system was originally fitted to the Harrier GR.3, the aircraft did not possess any passive defensive mechanisms, such as chaff or flares, although a number of GR.3s were subsequently modified to carry the Tracor ALE-40 chaff and flare dispenser on the lower rear fuselage and the wing pylon-mounted Phimat chaff dispensers.

A second production order for new-build Harrier GR.3s was placed in 1978, to cover attrition, and the Pegasus Mk 103 engine, LRMTS and PWR were also fitted to the two-seat Harriers, which were then redesignated as T.4s.

A further sub-variant of the T.4 is the T.4A, used exclusively by the Operational Conversion Unit. Most of the two-seaters used by No 233 OCU do not have the same need for the LRMTS and, in order to save on costs and weight, a so-called lightweight version of the T.4, known as the T.4A, was converted to this standard. The Harrier GR.3 continued to serve with the four frontline Squadrons until 1977. In that year, it was decided to re-locate the three RAF Germany-based squadrons from RAF Wildenrath, one of the 'Clutch' bases near the German/Dutch border, to RAF Gutersloh, the nearest RAF base to the former East German border. The three RAF Germany Harrier squadrons were merged into two larger squadrons and 20 Squadron exchanged its Harriers for Jaguars, and relocated to RAF Bruggen. While the RAF Germany Harrier Squadrons continued to exercise their primary war role in support of the British Army of the Rhine, the UK-based No 1 (Fighter) Squadron was committed to a much wider mission as part of the SACEUR Strategic Reserve. As such, the squadron had to be ready to deploy to either the northern or southern flanks of NATO, which saw the squadron frequently deployed overseas. The squadron was also committed to more general deployment anywhere in the world and the RAF regularly detached aircraft to fly from British aircraft carriers to refine the process that had been started back in 1963. They also deployed aircraft on long-range flights using air-to-air refuelling.

In 1975 the need for rapid deployment became a reality and 1(F) Sqn was given a short-notice requirement to deploy six aircraft to Belize, previously the colony of British Honduras, to counter threats from a potentially hostile neighbour, Guatemala. The six aircraft staged nonstop across the Atlantic then south through America to arrive in Belize, where they immediately started to fly operational missions. Some 15 years later the RAF Harrier detachment was still in place, operating Harrier GR.3s and having acquired its own identity as No 1417 Flight.

In between these periods, No 1(F) Squadron became embroiled in what became one of the most auspicious periods of its unit history, when it joined the British Task Force to counter the Argentinian invasion of the Falkland Islands in 1982. No 1(F) Sqn was put on alert in April 1982, principally to act as a reinforcement for the Sea Harriers of the Fleet Air Arm, which were embarked aboard HMS *Hermes* and *Invincible* and were envisaged to suffer high attrition rates. Preparation for the anticipated operation actually involved the entire RAF Harrier Force and 16 single-seat GR.3s, with good hours between major overhauls, were selected for extended operations at sea.

The need to operate permanently from the decks of aircraft carriers and in an interceptor role, new to the Harrier GR.3, required a number of modifications to be carried out to the airframe at short notice. An I-band transponder, compatible with that fitted to the Sea Harrier FRS.1, was mounted in a chin fairing under the nose to facilitate approaches to the carrier. In addition, the necessary wiring and switches to allow the GR3 to carry and launch a pair of AIM-9G Sidewinder air-to-air missiles from the outer wing pylons was also completed. Other armament

Harrier T.4 ZB600/Z of 233 OCU sits on the ramp at RAF Wittering. Note the 25Kva 'Houchin', which provides a ground power supply to the aircraft prior to start-up.

developments for the GR.3 included clearance to carry the 1,000lb Paveway Laser Guided Bomb (LGB). The aforementioned Tracor ALE-40 chaff/flare dispensers were also fitted to 10 of the Harrier GR.3s and the undercarriage outriggers on all the aircraft were also fitted with shackles, to allow the GR.3 to be tied down to the carrier deck.

To reduce saltwater corrosion of the airframe at sea, some of the special sealing and drainage techniques developed for the Sea Harrier were also applied. The RAF GR.3s were eventually embarked on HMS *Hermes* after initially deploying to the staging post at Ascension Island and transferring to the ill-fated container ship *Atlantic Conveyor*. The GR.3s completed an intensive work up in their new interception role before it was decided that Sea Harrier attrition was low enough to allow the RAF aircraft to revert to their more familiar role of ground attack or low-level reconnaissance.

The Harrier GR.3s operated from HMS *Hermes* for most of the Falklands campaign, conducting a wide range of CAS and battlefield reconnaissance missions in support of the Task Force. Later, they operated from a rudimentary forward operating base at San Carlos before eventually re-locating to the airfield at Port Stanley. A new Harrier detachment became permanently based at RAF Stanley (as the airfield became known), and was manned from all three frontline squadrons. In time the detachment was officially renamed as No 1453 Flight and it continued to provide air defence for the Falkland Islands until May 1985, when the new airport, RAF Mount Pleasant, opened and the McDonnell Douglas Phantom assumed responsibility for the islands' air defence.

The signing of a Memorandum of Understanding between Hawker Siddeley Aviation Ltd (to become part of British Aerospace) and the McDonnell Douglas Corporation during the early production of the AV-8A Harrier Mk 50 provided the impetus for new research and development into a second-generation Harrier family. By March 1975, the UK Government had abandoned ideas for a joint project and British Aerospace, which had subsumed the original Hawker Siddeley company, decided to limit its studies into the next generation of a Harrier. Meanwhile, the US Government and McDonnell Douglas, encouraged by the USMC, continued to investigate a limited upgrade of the AV-8A. The AV-8A had proved itself ideally suited to the USMC *raison d'être* for fixed-wing operations, providing the service with a fixed-wing CAS capability from ships and rudimentary forward operating bases. The Harrier's V/STOL capability was deemed to be extremely practical and the main limitations on the aircraft's operational capabilities centred on its limited payload and range. The US authorities decided to look at a 'big wing' derivative of the aircraft, shunning a major change in powerplant (deemed to be too costly), and seeking instead limited improvements to the existing Pegasus series and aerodynamic improvements to the basic airframe.

Following the formal 'divorce' from British Aerospace in 1975, McDonnell Douglas offered the USMC the AV-8B, which featured an all-new mainplane, with enlarged span and area. The aerofoil section was considerably thicker, providing more internal fuel capacity, and was linked with larger slotted flaps, which provided improved Short Take Off performance. Another radical departure from the first-generation Harrier design was the use of a carbon-fibre composite material in the construction of the flying surfaces, which also provided a valuable saving in the all-up weight of the aircraft. The increase in the wingspan enabled the AV-8B to be equipped with two additional stores pylons. The rear portion of the fuselage retained most of the design features of the original although it was enlarged and featured more prominent under-fuselage strakes and a retractable air dam. This significantly improved the aircraft's handling characteristics, particularly during the critical so-called transitional phase from conventional to vertical flight. Another significant design change involved the movement of the outrigger undercarriage from the wing-tips to a new inboard position, which greatly improved the aircraft's ability to taxi and operate from narrow strips and public roads.

The Pegasus Mk 105, a derivative of the Mk 104 fitted to the Sea Harrier, was selected to power the new aircraft. For the purposes of operating in field conditions, its reliability and maintainability were more important than any increase in thrust.

The front fuselage was almost entirely redesigned in order to allow the USMC to take advantage of the massive changes in technology and expand the range of roles and missions that the aircraft could undertake. The pilot now benefited from a raised and enlarged cockpit and bubble canopy, which provided him with excellent rearward vision, overcoming a significant weakness of the first-generation AV-8A. Another distinctive change to the forward fuselage design included the installation of a retractable inflight-refuelling probe, which replaced the fixed device used on first-generation Harriers; the entire probe installation and fairing could be removed when required. Other obvious changes to the overall design include a larger fin, squarer 'hot' and 'cold' exhaust nozzles and large Leading Edge Root Extensions (LERXs), which form part of the Lift Improvement Devices (LIDs).

The prototype YAV-8B, a converted AV-8A, first flew from McDonnell Douglas' St Louis facility in November 1978 and the flight testing of the first full-scale development AV-8B took place three years later, in November 1981.

During the early part of the development phase for the AV-8B, the British Government, having declared its independence from the joint programme, was pursuing its own second-generation Harrier. The original Harrier GR.5 was to be a big-winged version of the basic GR.3. The original plan envisaged a combination of new-build aircraft and the conversion of a number of existing Harrier GR.3 airframes, all utilizing a new metal large wing. Owing to a number of problems, mainly associated with the increased weight of the new aircraft and the fact that delays in a proposed start state would have an impact on the viability of converting in-service GR.3s with high airframe hours, the project became less attractive. The economics of such a small production run, accounting for no more than 60 new-build aircraft, also suggested that it could become cost-prohibitive.

Initially hesitant, the British Government and MOD Air Staff eventually accepted the improvements that would come with a second-generation Harrier family when McDonnell Douglas demonstrated the considerable advances that had been made with their AV-8B Harrier II. Given the modest number of aircraft that would eventually be ordered for the Royal Air Force, and realizing that the US company would almost certainly secure orders for more than 400 aircraft, the British Government entered into an agreement with the US company – a single basic design would be shared by each country, with each contributing significant parts of each aircraft. In August 1981 the UK Government abandoned its plans for an 'independent' second-generation Harrier and signed a Memorandum of Understanding with the US Government to buy a variant of the AV-8B Harrier II to meet the RAF specification. The initial UK order for sixty AV-8Bs, to be known in RAF service as the Harrier GR.5, was placed in August 1982.

As a result of these delays, the USMC received its aircraft into frontline service some four years before the RAF. The first aircraft went to MCAS Cherry Point to begin the task of replacing the AV-8As with VMAT-203, the training unit receiving early examples of the new Harrier. VMA-331 'Bumblebees', a former A-4 Skyhawk unit, became the first frontline unit to receive the aircraft and became operational on the new type in January 1985. Two other squadrons at Cherry Point – VMA-231 'Ace of Spades' and VMA-542 'Flying Tigers' – received the aircraft with full conversion completed by the summer of 1986. By this stage it had already been decided to expand the number of frontline USMC squadrons flying the Harrier and deliveries were switched to Yuma on the west coast, where VMA-513 'Flying Nightmares' received its aircraft in August 1986. Four former USMC A-4 Skyhawk units – VMA-211 'Wake Island Avengers', VMA-214 'Black Sheep', VMA-223 'Bulldogs' and VMA-311 'Tomcats' – received the balance of the USMC AV-8Bs between 1986 and 1989.

USMC AV-8Bs acquitted themselves extremely well during Operation *Desert Storm* in early 1991, during which they performed a wide range of roles.

Since then, they have seen further action in a number of theatres including NATO air operations over Bosnia and Kosovo.

Delivery of the RAF's GR.5s was further delayed by problems with some of the UK-sourced equipment that had been specified for the aircraft. The AV-8B and GR.5 aircraft had much in common although there were a number of differences, particularly with the avionics and weapons fit. The early avionics fit on the AV-8B included the Litton ASN-130 Inertial Navigation System (INS), the Smiths HUD and a Hughes Angle Rate Bombing Set (ARBS). The RAF GR.5 was initially equipped with a Ferranti FIN 1075 INS in lieu of the Litton equipment although this had to be abandoned in favour of the latter system shortly after the aircraft entered service. The cockpit is equipped with Hands-On-Throttle and Stick (HOTAS), allowing the pilot to control virtually all of the mission-essential components without removing his hands from the control column. The AV-8Bs of USMC and, later, of the Spanish Armada and Italian Navy, are equipped with a single General Electric GAU-12/U 25mm rotary cannon mounted in one of the two under-fuselage pods. The RAF replaced this gun on the GR.5 with a pair of indigenous 25mm Aden cannons but continual problems with the performance and reliability of the weapon has now forced its withdrawal from service. The Marconi Zeus internal ECM was initially fitted, along with ALE-40 chaff/flares in an under-fuselage dispenser similar to those fitted on Operation *Corporate* GR.3s for the Falkland Islands campaign.

Other RAF changes to the original AV-8B specification included strengthened panels on the wing leading edge and around the intake lips, and the fitting of a Martin-Baker Mk 12 zero-zero seat in place of the US Navy/USMC standard Stencel series of seats. The MB Mk 12 seat fit in the GR.5 also produced some initial problems when the aircraft was introduced into service. While all AV-8Bs have seven stores pylons, the RAF GR.5s were equipped with two additional stations specifically designed to carry two self-defence AIM-9 Sidewinder AAMs, without taking up valuable space on any of the existing stores pylons. As a result, RAF GR.5s were, on entry into service, more comprehensively equipped than their USMC counterparts, albeit at greater financial cost and with a loss in commonality.

The first Harrier GR.5 was handed over to the RAF in July 1987 and first deliveries to the Operational Conversion Unit at RAF Wittering took place in the summer of 1988. By this time the RAF had ordered a total of ninety-six aircraft, including two development aircraft, the initial order for sixty

and a follow-on order for thirty-four aircraft, placed in April 1988. The rapid development of operational equipment for Royal Air Force Harriers resulted in the re-designation of the aircraft, as GR.5A, before deliveries could be completed. The first GR.5A was flown in 1989 and No 3(F) Squadron became the first operational squadron to convert to this mark in March of that year.

In the mean time, two further developments of the second-generation Harrier were under way, including a night attack version of the aircraft. This variant had first been revealed in 1984 and first flew in 1987. It was equipped with a GEC FLIR sensor mounted prominently above the nose. In the cockpit, a new wide-angle HUD was combined with new head-down displays, a digital moving map display and lighting compatible with the use of Night Vision Goggles (NVGs). Further equipment changes to this variant for RAF service, including the installation of two antennae under the extreme nose, associated with the Zeus fitment, resulted in another change of designation – to Harrier GR Mk 7. Externally, the variant does not differ greatly from the GR.5A.

The Harrier GR.7 remains the definitive RAF single-seat version and has continued to receive a number of modifications in the light of operational experience. Arriving too late into operational service to be deployed alongside its USMC counterparts during the Gulf War, in 1991, the RAF's second-generation Harriers have since been employed in a wide range of Out of Area operations requiring the use of flexible air power. The aircraft has acquitted itself extremely well during operations over Northern Iraq as part of Operation *Warden* and in the Balkans during a number of UN- or NATO-sponsored air campaigns over the former Yugoslavia, Bosnia and Kosovo. The aircraft can now operate with the latest range of laser-guided munitions and has limited laser designation capability following successful trials with TIALD. The aircraft is cleared to use the Paveway II and III series of LGBs and, more recently, the AGM-65G2 Maverick. The aircraft has also acquired new tactical reconnaissance capabilities with the new Vinten pod. External changes to the airframe have been minimal apart from the fitment of the Bofors BOL chaff system to the rear end of the Sidewinder stores pylons.

In service, the Harrier GR.7 continued to equip three operational squadrons – No 1(F) Sqn at RAF Wittering and No 3(F) and IV(AC) Sqn at RAF Laarbruch in Germany. With the staged withdrawal of the RAF from Germany, the Harriers of the two latter squadrons returned to RAF Cottesmore, Rutland, during the course of 1999.

In April 2000, and following the culmination of work under the Strategic Defence Review of UK Forces, it was decided to combine the Harrier GR.7s of the RAF with the Sea Harriers of the Fleet Air Arm in one unified command, to be known as Joint Force Harrier. As a result, the RAF Harrier Force now find themselves deployed aboard the aircraft carriers of the Royal Navy on a regular basis as part of the organic carrier air group. This concept was successfully proven early in 2001 when a joint Harrier force deployed to Sierra Leone in support of ground forces. It is likely that a similar force may become engaged in air operations over Afghanistan.

Operating alongside the single-seat GR.7s are 13 two-seat Harrier T.10 trainer aircraft, which are based on the TAV-8B but are fully combat-capable. The majority of T.10s are operated by No 20 (Reserve) Squadron, the Operational Conversion Unit at RAF Wittering, although each of the front-line squadrons retains at least one airframe. Currently, all of the frontline squadrons, 1(F), 3(F) and IV(AC), are based at RAF Cottesmore, with 20 (R) squadron remaining at the original 'Home of the Harrier', RAF Wittering.

The second McDonnell Douglas development of the AV-8B Harrier II involved the installation of a radar and more advanced avionics suite to meet the increasingly complex demands of the USMC and the Spanish and Italian naval air arms. The AV-8B Harrier II Plus programme, as it was dubbed, was launched in September 1990. It sought to combine the installation of the Hughes AN/APG-65 pulse-Doppler radar, similar to that fitted to the F/A-18A Hornet, with the ability to carry and use a wide range of advanced weapons systems, including the AIM-120 AMRAAM and the new-generation AGM-65G2 Maverick, while retaining full night attack capability. For the first time in its association with the Harrier family, the USMC enjoyed beyond visual range capability for both air-to-air and air-to-surface weapons systems, which was deemed to be crucial to the aircraft's survivability in modern air battle scenarios. Three of the eight USMC AV-8B frontline squadrons have subsequently re-equipped with the more capable Harrier II Plus aircraft.

Two other air arms now operate the second-generation AV-8B Harrier in a number of guises. Spain signed a contract for twelve AV-8Bs in March 1983. The aircraft, to be known as VA.2 Matador IIs,

BAe Harrier GR.7 wearing the earlier overall grey colour scheme adopted by the RAF Harrier force employed on Operation *Warden* duties over Northern Iraq in the mid-1990s. The aircraft wears temporary 'W' codes on the fin, signifying its role in Operation *Warden*, and is devoid of Squadron markings. It is fitted with a pair of AIM-9 Sidewinders and a Phimat pod for self-defence and also carries a W.Vinten tactical reconnaissance pod on the centreline pylon for surveillance purposes over the Northern Iraq/Turkish border area. (Photo: copyright BAe Systems plc)

General view of a Sea Harrier of 800 Naval Air Squadron taxiing on to an Operational Readiness Platform. The aircraft is fitted with two 30mm Aden gun pods, 100 imperial gallon drop tanks and a pair of AIM-9 Sidewinder acquisition rounds. Note also the bolt-on inflight-refuelling probe. The 'N' code on the tail indicates that this aircraft was part of the HMS *Invincible* Carrier Air Group.

are now more commonly referred to as EAV-8Bs. The new aircraft were delivered in September 1987 and equipped Escaudrilla 009, replacing the surviving AV-8A(S)s that had previously equipped Escaudrilla 008. The aircraft, shore-based at Rota, frequently operated aboard the new aircraft carrier *Principe de Asturias* (which entered service in 1989), as well as the Second World War vintage carrier *Dedalo*. Under a tripartite agreement signed in 1990, the surviving AV-8Bs were converted to Harrier II Plus standard and were joined by eight new-build Harrier II Pluses and a single TAV-8B two-seat trainer.

Italy became the second European nation to operate the McDonnell Douglas version of the AV-8B when it took the historic decision to allow the Marina Militaire to operate fixed-wing aircraft. This marked the end of a 52-year ban, imposed during the pre-Second World War Fascist era. Following government approval in 1989, the Italian Navy took immediate delivery of two TAV-8B trainers and began the long task of training Italian Navy pilots in fixed-wing operations. A total of 16 Harrier II Pluses were ordered and the first of these aircraft were delivered in 1994. The aircraft are operated by 1 Gruppo Aereo (1 Grupaer) from Grottaglie, close to the port of Taranto, from where the Italian Navy's aircraft carrier *Giuseppe Garibaldi* operates. Shortly after their entry into service the Italian Navy AV-8Bs flew in support of UN operations in Somalia and have been involved in a wide range of NATO air operations and exercises.

The Sea Harrier

The Navy can trace its involvement with jet V/STOL operations as far back as 1963, when the Hawker Siddeley test pilots operated the first P.1127 from an aircraft carrier, HMS *Ark Royal*, at sea. An early Admiralty requirement for a jet V/STOL fighter, abandoned on the grounds of cost, was to simmer for some years although the RAF conducted a number of trials with one of its Harriers in 1969 to prove the role of air support for amphibious landing operations. Following the earlier cancellation of large fleet aircraft carriers for the Royal Navy, it became clear that conventional fleet air arm fixed-wing operations were likely to cease when the remaining fleet carriers were decommissioned. The Admiralty consequently planned a new class of ship, known as the anti-submarine cruiser, from which it was originally envisaged that only rotary-wing aircraft would operate. This particular type of ship went through several different classifications, including through-deck cruiser and command cruiser, as well as picking up a new requirement for a novel ski-ramp facility from which to operate fully laden jet V/STOL aircraft, from any service, if the need arose.

The first ship, HMS *Invincible*, was ordered in 1973 and launched four years later, in 1977. During the intervening years, the Ministry of Defence reconsidered its earlier policy on the future of naval aviation and reversed its decision to make the Fleet Air Arm a helicopter-only Service. As a result, Hawker Siddeley was contracted, in 1975, to produce twenty-four Sea

Harrier aircraft, to be operated from the new *Invincible* class cruisers.The aircraft was designed to an Admiralty requirement, which called for an air interception capability against long-range maritime patrol and ship-based fighters, surface attack against ships or shore targets and reconnaissance. The Sea Harrier FRS.1 (fighter, reconnaissance, strike) was, as far as possible, to be based on the existing GR.3 airframe, although it would incorporate a radar for the aircraft's primary role of air defence and use new materials in its construction to lessen the effects of corrosion while operating at sea for extended periods. Unsurprisingly, given the air interception role, the design of the forward fuselage was altered radically to accommodate the new radar and avionics suite. The cockpit was raised by almost a foot to provide more space for equipment under the floor and the cockpit layout was revised. The pilot's view was improved by the fitting of an all-new bubble canopy over the raised cockpit area.

The heart of the new aircraft was a Ferranti Blue Fox I-band pulse-modulated radar designed for air-to-air interception and air-to-surface search and strike. This was fitted behind a pointed radome in a folding nose, specified to allow the aircraft to fit on the lifts of the existing *Invincible* Class aircraft carriers. A Smiths Industries HUD was also incorporated into the design, combining radar displays with a Weapons Aiming Computer (WAC). Another Ferranti product, the self-aligning attitude reference platform was also fitted to provide all the navigation and endurance functions.

Primary armament for the air defence role was to be a pair of AIM-9 Sidewinder AAMs mounted on the outer wing pylons. The Fleet Air Arm also envisaged the retention of the two 30mm Aden guns in the under-fuselage pods for both the air defence and surface attack role. Rolls-Royce refined the Pegasus engine, eliminating as many magnesium components as possible, to produce the Mk 104, rated to a similar specification as the GR.3's Mk 103.

Parallel work on the development of the so-called ski-jump launch facility, which was incorporated into all the carriers likely to operate the Sea Harrier, resulted in a facility that greatly increased the diminutive Sea Harrier's effectiveness aboard ship. In practice the gains were dramatic. Using the ski-ramp the Sea Harrier could take off in 50 per cent of the distance required for a conventional flat-deck launch or could carry a 30 per cent increase in weapons and fuel load.

The Sea Harrier made its first flight at Dunsfold in August 1978 and by this time the Fleet Air Arm had increased its initial order to 34 aircraft. The Royal Navy took delivery of its first aircraft in June 1979 and formed an Intensive Flying Trials Unit, No 700A Naval Air Squadron, to rapidly build up experience on this new aircraft.

No 700A Squadron re-formed as 899 Squadron, the Sea Harrier Headquarters and Training Squadron, at RNAS Yeovilton on 31 March 1980. Sea Harrier FRS.1s were delivered to No 800 Squadron, the first operational squadron, almost simultaneously, and No 801 Squadron received its aircraft in January 1981. Less than 18 months later, the Sea Harriers of the Fleet Air Arm faced their first operational test when they formed the core of the UK's organic air power aboard the ships of the British Task Force launched to counter the invasion of the Falkland Islands by the Argentinian military, in April 1982. No 800 Naval Air Squadron (NAS) embarked 12 Sea Harriers aboard HMS *Hermes* and they were shortly followed by No 801 NAS with eight aircraft aboard HMS *Invincible*; these were the only two carriers available for operational deployment in April 1982. Shortly after the Task Force sailed, the Royal Navy decided to re-form a third operational Sea Harrier unit and 809 NAS was commissioned at RNAS Yeovilton on 8 April 1982. The squadron deployed a further eight Sea Harriers to Ascension Island, via West Africa, before joining the Harrier GR.3s of No 1(F) Squadron RAF aboard *Atlantic Conveyor* for the long journey to the South Atlantic.

While these deployments were taking place, development work was going on to provide the Sea Harrier with in-service enhancements, including the design of a twin-Sidewinder launcher to double the aircraft's capability to carry the AAM missile. Clearance to carry a range of ground attack weapons, including the BL755 cluster bomb, was also sought and the Tracor ALE-40 chaff/flare dispenser was mounted in the rear fuselage for self-defence. Early in the Falklands campaign the Sea Harriers alone were employed in both the air defence role, flying Combat Air Patrol above the Task Force, and in the low-level ground attack and reconnaissance role, pending the arrival of the Harrier GR.3s from Ascension Island. After a period of intensive air activity and the denial of the airfield at Part Stanley to Argentinian interceptors and attack aircraft, the Sea Harriers gained air superiority over the Total Exclusion Zone (TEZ). With the arrival of the Harrier GR.3s and more Sea Harriers, the Royal Navy was able to divert some of its assets to the prosecution of the campaign on the ground in support of land forces.

Although the Fleet Air Arm lost six Sea Harriers during Operation *Corporate*, not one of these was attributable to air combat. On its return from the South Atlantic the Fleet Air Arm reverted to two operational squadrons with the disbandment of 809 NAS. The British Government ordered a further 14 Sea Harriers in July 1982, to make up losses and to provide each of the operational squadrons with an increased complement of aircraft. A further order in 1984 brought total UK procurement of the Sea Harrier FRS.1 to 57 aircraft. On their return to more routine operations, the Sea Harriers began the task of operating with Sea Eagle, the new active radar anti-shipping missile, which had first entered service with the RAF's Buccaneer maritime attack squadrons, replacing the Martel. The Sea Eagle gave the Sea Harrier a further role to add to its impressive tally, allowing the aircraft to attack heavily armed naval vessels from outside the range of their fixed weapons systems.

Like the Royal Air Force before it, the Fleet Air Arm introduced the Sea Harrier into service without the benefit of a two-seat trainer. A Harrier T.4A was included in the order for the first batch of Sea Harriers and operated as part of 233 OCU at RAF Wittering, since all Harrier pilots, regardless of service, underwent their conversion training at this Unit. The Navy later ordered a batch of three T.4Ns (N for 'navalized'), for service with its indigenous training unit, 899 NAS, at RNAS Yeovilton. Externally similar to the RAF's T4A, these aircraft were pure trainers; they were not radar-equipped and are not, therefore, carrier-compatible.

Following its huge success during the Falklands campaign the Sea Harrier could have been reasonably expected to gain a number of foreign orders. So far, however, India is the only nation to have operated the aircraft, and in very limited quantities. The Indian Government ordered a total of 16 single-seat FRS.51s and three two-seat T.60s together with the Sea Eagle anti-shipping missile system. The FRS.51 is almost identical to the original FRS.1 apart from some internal equipment changes and the ability to carry the Matra M550 Magic AAM in lieu of the AIM-9. The aircraft equip one frontline unit, No 300 'Tiger' Squadron, and 'B' Flight of No 551 Squadron, the Indian Navy fixed-wing training squadron, both based at Goa-Dabolim naval air base on the west coast. The Sea Harriers of 300 Sqn are regularly deployed as part of a mixed carrier air group aboard the two ex-Royal Navy aircraft carriers of the Indian Navy. Both INS *Viraat* (formerly HMS *Hermes)* and INS *Vikrant* (formerly HMS *Hercules*) are equipped with ski-ramps.

As with every other air campaign in history, lessons were learned during Operation *Corporate* and it became clear that, notwithstanding its success against a numerically superior foe, the Sea Harrier FRS.1 suffered from a fundamental tactical weakness. The Blue Fox radar was unable to target more than one opposing aircraft simultaneously. A Mid Life Update (MLU) for the Sea Harrier FRS.1 fleet was approved, which provided for a new advanced multi-mode pulse-Doppler Blue Vixen radar, linked to new weapons systems including the AIM-120 Advanced Medium Range Air-to-Air Missile (AMRAAM) and the BAe Sea Eagle sea-skimming anti-ship missile.

Externally, the most noticeable difference between the two Sea Harrier variants is the the slightly shorter, more rounded nose that is required to accommodate the much larger Blue Vixen radar suite, and the re-location of the pitot tube to the leading edge of the fin. Two other changes involved a new 14in fuselage insert, principally to accommodate additional avionics and self-defence systems, and extended wing-tips. The cockpit area is now dominated by two multi-purpose display screens and most of the weapon system controls are positioned on a new upfront control panel or on the Hands On Throttle and Stick (HOTAS). More subtle changes to the airframe included the addition of a wing fence and the incorporation of a kinked leading edge, with the associated elimination of the dogtooth and one of the original 12 vortex generators on the leading edge of the mainplane. These aerodynamic changes helped to improve the performance of the wing at high angles of attack with drop tanks fitted. The fuselage-mounted ram air turbine was deleted from the new aircraft and power was provided by the Pegasus Mk 106 engine, a navalized variant of the Mk 105 used in the AV-8B second-generation Harrier II. Fuselage- and wing-mounted stores pylons have also been re-designed to house the new Hughes AIM-120 AMRAAM, BAe Alarm Anti-Radiation Missiles and the new generation of Paveway Laser Guided Bombs (LGBs).

Two development conversions from FRS.1 aircraft were ordered in 1985 and the first Sea Harrier FRS.2 was flown on 19 September 1988. In December 1988 the MOD awarded a contract for the conversion of 31 Sea Harrier FRS.1 aircraft between 1991 and 1994 and in March 1990 a follow-on order for 10 new build aircraft was announced to supplement the original FRS.1 fleet which had dropped to 39 aircraft as a result of in-service attrition.

The 'new' Sea Harrier, by now re-designated as the F/A-2 Sea Harrier, has re-equipped the three existing Squadrons at RNAS Yeovilton. Like its RAF brethren, it has been actively involved in a wide range of worldwide operations, including the NATO air operations over the Adriatic and, to a lesser extent, with coalition forces in the Middle East. More recently, the Harrier F/A-2s, now part of the Joint Harrier Force commanded by HQ 3 Group at RAF High Wycombe, have conducted joint embarked air operations with RAF Harrier GR.7s in Sierra Leone and been involved during major joint force exercises to test the Joint Rapid Reaction Force (JRRF) concept. The aircraft is now fully integrated with the AIM-120 AMRAAM missile system, providing the Fleet Air Arm with one of the most capable interceptors in the current NATO inventory. The aircraft has lost its Sea Eagle anti-shipping missile capability but has gained an enhanced podded reconnaissance system to supplement the fixed F95 camera, and JTIDS, which finally allows the aircraft to interface with the E-3D AWACs of the Royal Air Force as well as components of a US Navy Battle Group.

These system enhancements should have allowed the aircraft to serve in the Fleet Air Arms until the first deliveries of the maritime version of the Joint Strike Fighter (JSF) are received later in the decade. In a controversial move that surprised many, however, the British government announced in 2002 the retirement of the Sea Harrier F/A-2 by 2006, which will bring to a premature end the long and distinguished career of this unique Fleet Air Arm aircraft.

There can be no doubt that the Harrier has proved to be a success story. In its 32-year operational history as the world's only true V/STOL fighter aircraft, it has served the air arms of five nations extremely successfully. The basic design has adapted well to the changes and advances in aircraft technology and to the ever-increasing demands of the operational environment in which the Harrier is expected to operate. The Harrier has now enjoyed a proven operational record in all of the various roles for which it has been procured and operated, and will continue to do so for many years.

A Sea Harrier F/A-2 comes to the hover before landing on an *Invincible* Class carrier 'somewhere in the Adriatic'. The aircraft, employed on Operation *Deny Flight*, the UN-sanctioned air operation over the former Yugoslavia during the mid-1990s, is carrying a single 1,000lb GP bomb on the centreline and a pair of drop tanks to extend its overland range. (Photo: copyright BAe Systems plc)

Early Harriers

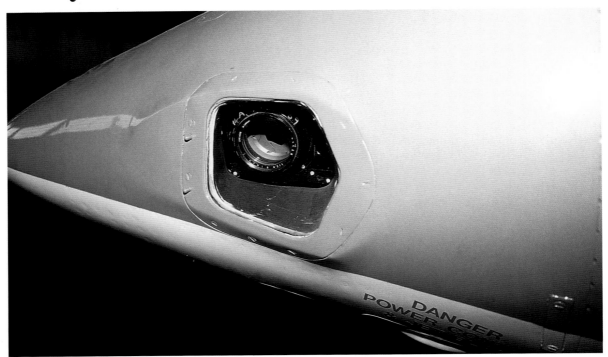

Two close-up views of the pointed nose of the original Hawker Siddeley Harrier GR.1 variant, which is partially preserved at RAF Wittering. The installation of a port-facing 70mm F95 camera provided the aircraft with a limited reconnaissance capability. Note also the demarcation line between the light aircraft grey undersurfaces and the upper surface camouflage scheme, and the style of red warning markings.

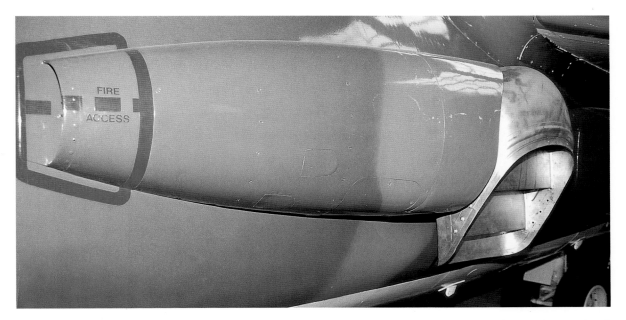

View of the fairing covering the forward (cold) jet exhaust nozzle – evidence of the structural differences of the Harrier variants through the years. This shape identifies this aircraft as one of the pre-production Harrier GR.1s. By the time production aircraft had entered service with 1(F) Sqn, the shape of this fairing had changed considerably. The red markings at the forward end of the fairing warn groundcrew of the presence of an auxiliary air intake.

BELOW: Two close-up photographs of the forward (cold) jet exhaust nozzle on the pre-production Harrier GR.1, which was common to all variants of the first-generation Harrier family.

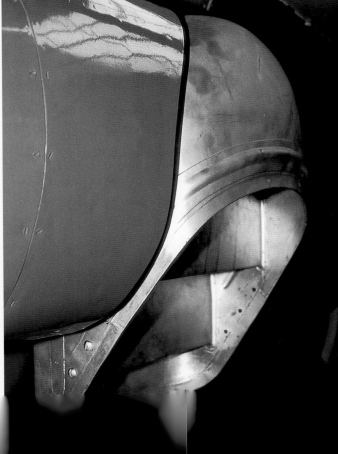

OPPOSITE PAGE: View down the main air intake of the pre-production Harrier GR.1, showing the massive fan of the Rolls-Royce Pegasus 6 Mk 101 engine that powered the early RAF Harrier.

The fuselage heat shield on the early pre-production Harrier GR.1 was an extremely simple piece of equipment, markedly different from the component found on production first-generation Harrier GR.1s. Note the complete absence of ribbing on the outer surfaces of the shield.

BELOW: A general view of British Aerospace Harrier GR.3 XW924/G, which has been preserved in 3(F) Sqn markings and currently resides outside the Squadron headquarters at RAF Cottesmore.

BAe Harrier GR.3 XZ990/3D of 233 OCU, on the flight line at RAF Wittering during the mid-1980s. The crew access ladder and position of the electrical cables from a shared 'splitter box', seen in the background, provide useful reference points for modellers wishing to produce a diorama. Note also the old-style 233 OCU markings, used before the unit was redesignated as 20(R) Sqn.

When this photograph was taken in 1990, this was one of the last remaining Harrier T.2s left in RAF service. The aircraft wears the old-style 233 OCU markings on the nose and is fitted with a pair of 100 imperial gallon drop tanks. Note also the position of the crew access ladder, fire extinguisher and ground earthing lead.

Harrier GR.5

ABOVE: This close-up view of an early Harrier GR.5 of 1(F) Sqn provides some useful detail on the distinctive nose featured on the first RAF examples of the second-generation Harrier II. The nose profile was dictated by a triangular housing for the MIRLS linescan reconnaissance system, which was never actually fitted to the aircraft. Note also the position of the fluorescent formation lighting strips under the cockpit and the inflight-refuelling probe, which has been deployed for display purposes.

BAe Harrier GR.5 about to start up at RAF Wittering. The aircraft is already showing signs of wear and tear, judging by the general condition of the paintwork and the number of flush rivets that have obviously been removed at some point to gain access to equipment.

BAe Harrier GR.5 ZD323/C of 233 OCU at RAF Wittering, shortly after delivery to the Unit. The aircraft is fitted with a full complement of weapons stores pylons although it appears to be carrying only a single acquisition round on the port outer pylon and a pair of 25mm Aden gun pods.

BELOW: This unusual view of a 1(F) Sqn Harrier GR.5A includes some useful reference material on the mainplane, weapons pylons and inflight-refuelling probe installation. Note also the demarcation line between the two shades of green camouflage, which is quite marked.

Harrier GR.7

A 1(F) Sqn Harrier GR.7 – note in particular the position of the auxiliary air intake doors, relative to gravity, and the open cockpit canopy on this single-seat variant. The position and style of the various markings that adorn the forward fuselage, and the contrast in camouflage greens is also noteworthy.

BELOW: Harrier GR.7 ZD329/H, sporting the markings of 20(R) Sqn, the Harrier OCU, taxies out to conduct a solo flying display at RAF Fairford during IAT '95. The two-tone green camouflage scheme was worn by Harrier GR.5/7s and T.10s when they first entered service in the late 1980s. The official colours were NATO Dark Green (BS381C.285) on upper surfaces, with Lichen Green (BS4800.12B21) on lower surfaces.

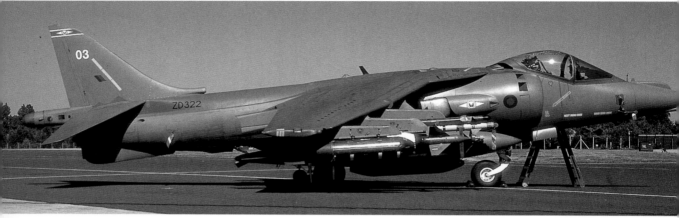

TOP: A fully laden Harrier GR.7 in the most recent, two-tone grey camouflage colour scheme of Dark Sea Grey (BS638) on upper surfaces and Dark Camouflage Grey (BS629) on lower surfaces. The second-generation Harrier had impressive load-carrying capabilities; this aircraft is fitted with a pair of 25mm Aden cannon pods and drop tanks. An AIM-9L Sidewinder, carried by the Harrier GR.7 as a self-defence weapon, occupies the missile pylon with a drill Paveway II LGB on the middle weapons pylon and a Hunting BL775 cluster bomb on the outer weapons pylon. A W. Vinten Vicon 18 Series 601 tactical reconnaissance pod can just be seen on the centreline fuselage pylon.

MIDDLE: Harrier GR.7 ZD322/03 of 1(F) Sqn with a full weapons load. Note the number of Remove Before Flights (RBF) tags.

BOTTOM: Rear three-quarter shot of a very clean Harrier GR.7 (ZD376/24) of 3(F) Sqn, then based at RAF Laarbruch in Germany. The demarcation line between the two-tone grey camouflage scheme is difficult to pick out, but the special flash underneath the cockpit canopy distinguishes this aircraft as belonging to the Squadron Commander. Judging by the lack of RBF tags, this aircraft is obviously being readied for a sortie, although the engine intake blanks are still in place.

Harrier GR.7s on the line at RAF Wittering. The aircraft nearest the camera wears the markings of IV(AC) Squadron, and carries a pair of drop tanks, Sidewinder acquisition rounds and Carrier Bomb Light Stores, colloquially known by RAF air- and ground crew as 'Ceeblees'. There are many protective blanks and RBF tags fitted to the aircraft. Note also the position of the small access doors on the lower air intake surfaces.

BELOW: A Harrier GR.7 on the line at RAF Wittering, giving a good view of the sizeable maintenance and crew access ladder that is used at the Harrier Main Operating Base. Note also the style and position of the various RBF tags that adorn this particular airframe.

Harrier GR.7 ZD378/26 of 20(R) Sqn was one of two aircraft to receive special tail markings for the 2001 air display season. Note the distinct lack of stores pylons on this particular aircraft, which has been stripped for flying display purposes, and the position of the fire extinguisher trolley in the foreground.

BELOW: Close-up of the GR.7 nose. The clear nose cap contains the dual-mode TV/laser target seeker/tracker of the AN/ASB-19 Angle Rate Bombing Set (ARBS). Below the nose are the twin housings for the Zeus ECM system.

Two views of a fully
laden IV(AC) Sqn Harrier
GR.7 sitting in a hide.
Note the deployed
inflight-refuelling probe,
which would normally be
stowed when the aircraft
is on the ground, and
the layout of the metal
tracking, used to aid the
movement of the aircraft
over soft ground.

This close-up view of the GR.7 shows the position of the GEC-Marconi Forward Looking Infra-Red (FLIR) fairing on the upper nose surfaces.

View showing the position of the yaw vane and small IFF blade aerial located on the upper nose surfaces of the Harrier GR.7.

Close-ups of the access steps *(above)* on the port side of the fuselage, and the pull-down step *(right)* adjacent to the main air intake. Note the dual-language rescue/safety markings, which confirm that this particular aircraft had served with 3(F) or IV(AC) Squadron at RAF Laarbruch in Germany.

TOP LEFT: General view of the starboard air intake. Note the thickness of the air intake lip and the demarcation line between the external camouflage colour and the gloss white finish to the inner surfaces of the intake.

TOP RIGHT: A closer look at the inner surfaces of the starboard air intake reveals the shape and colour of the massive fan blades of the Rolls-Royce Pegasus engine. Note also the style and position of the flushed rivets in the intake construction, the location of the engine temperature sensor on the intake wall, and the yellow primer coloured 'patches'. The white inner finish soon turns semi-gloss with use.

Close-up view of the engine temperature sensor on the inner 'wall' of the huge starboard air intake.

BOTTOM RIGHT: A distinguishing feature on all marks of Harrier, the auxiliary intake doors are located on the outer surfaces of the air intakes. Note the demarcation line between the two shades of camouflage grey.

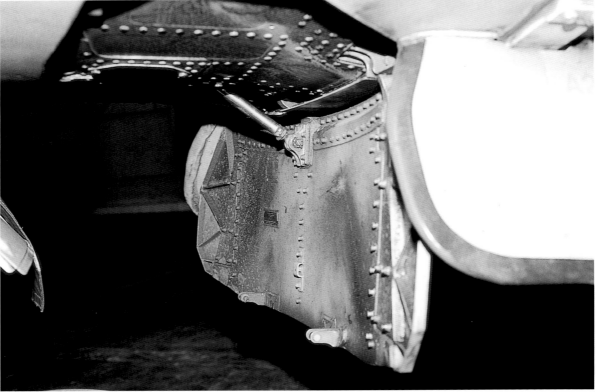

Two views of the retractable lift augmentation cross-dam that forms part of the Lift Improvement Device (LID) on the Harrier II family. The air dam door, which is located just behind the nose undercarriage bay, between the lateral strakes, is subject to considerable discoloration in service.

The blade-shaped fairing, located on the lower surfaces of the port engine air intake, has been a distinctive feature on all Harrier and Sea Harrier variants.

BELOW: Close-up of the aerodynamic fairing for the forward exhaust nozzle. Note the position of the auxiliary air intake, outlined in red, and the fuel dump pipe, located on the lower surfaces of the fairing. All of the current RAF Harrier Squadrons use this fairing for their distinctive Unit markings. In this case, the insignia belongs to 20(R) Sqn, the Harrier OCU.

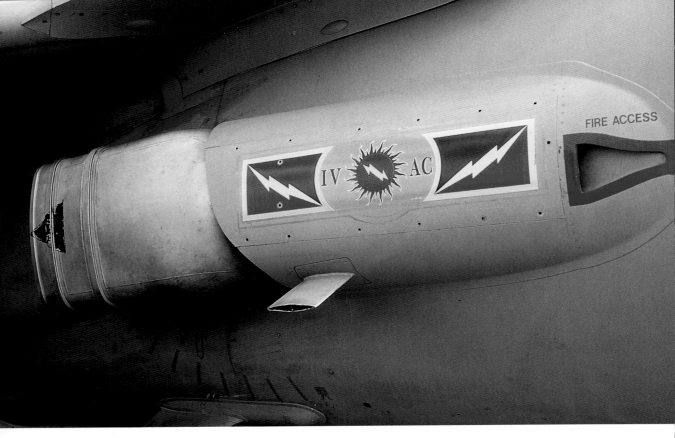

This general view of the starboard air intake area shows the position of the aerodynamic fairing in relation to the leading edge of the mainplane and the forward exhaust nozzle.

BELOW: Close-up of the port air intake fairing, showing, in detail, the Unit markings of IV(AC) Sqn, one of the three frontline RAF Harrier Squadrons, based at RAF Cottesmore.

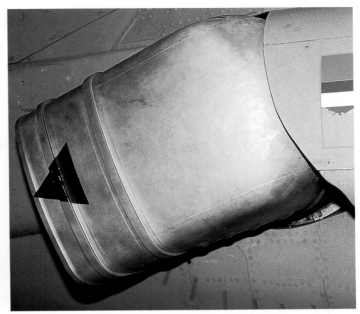

ABOVE: The forward zero-scarf (fan-air) swivelling exhaust nozzle in two different positions. Note the black triangle marking *(above right)*, applied to some aircraft, which aids observations of the position of the nozzle and the colour of the forward exhaust nozzles.

The heat exchanger ram air intakes are located on the sides of the elongated cockpit housing on the T.10 variant. On the GR.7, these intakes lie on top of the air intake adjacent to the cockpit canopy and the Leading-Edge Root Extension (LERX).

BELOW: The main receptacle of the demountable flight-refuelling probe, which is fitted to the upper surfaces of the port air intake.

The rear (hot-stream) swivelling exhaust nozzle and fuselage heat shield. The internal views of the exhaust nozzle are particularly useful. Note the considerable amount of exhaust build-up on the heat shield.

Rear view of the large lateral fuselage strake, which forms part of the Lift Improvement Device (LID) system on the Harrier II series of aircraft. These strakes are removed when the aircraft is roled to carry the twin 25mm Aden gun pods.

BELOW: Close-up of the heat exchanger exhaust, located just forward of the leading edge of the all-moving tailplane. Note also the demarcation line between the two-grey camouflage scheme.

DANGER
JET BLAST

OPPOSITE PAGE:
TOP: Upper view of the port Leading Edge Root Extension (LERX), which forms part of the LID system.

BOTTOM: The control surfaces of the Harrier are not normally deployed while the aircraft is at rest on the ground. This photograph shows the large carbon-fibre composite slotted flap in the fully deployed position, during the routine servicing of a T.10 airframe.

THIS PAGE:
TOP: General view of the starboard wing-tip of the Harrier GR.7, clearly showing, in the centre, the upper surface vent for the roll control reaction air valve, which is duplicated on the lower surfaces of the wing. The fuel dump pipe can be seen at the rear, and, on the leading edge, the navigation light and RWR antenna. Note also the fluorescent wing-tip formation lighting strips.

BOTTOM: A clear depiction of the design of the ventral airbrake panel and the hydraulic jack. The internal surfaces of the air brake fairing are finished in camouflage grey while the hydraulic jack is gloss white, although in service this soon turns to a semi-gloss 'dirty' white. Note also the location of the ventral navigation/formation light.

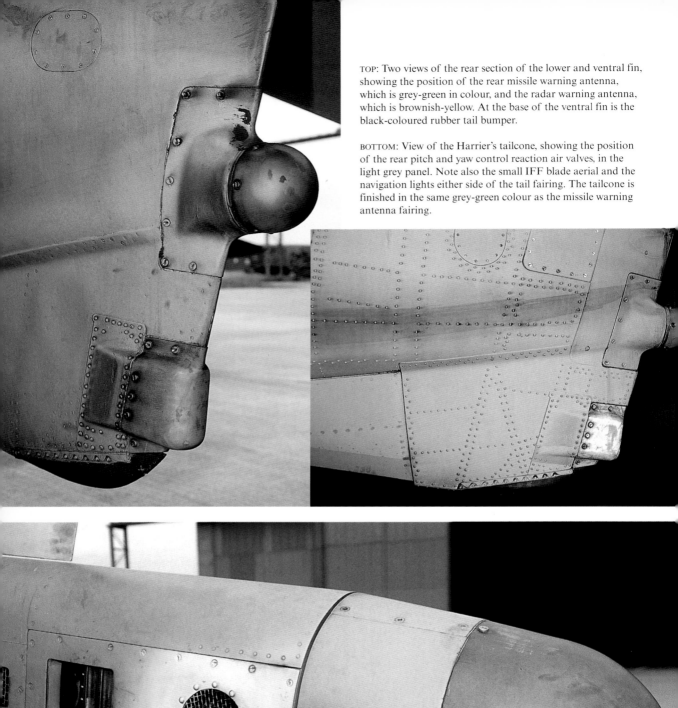

TOP: Two views of the rear section of the lower and ventral fin, showing the position of the rear missile warning antenna, which is grey-green in colour, and the radar warning antenna, which is brownish-yellow. At the base of the ventral fin is the black-coloured rubber tail bumper.

BOTTOM: View of the Harrier's tailcone, showing the position of the rear pitch and yaw control reaction air valves, in the light grey panel. Note also the small IFF blade aerial and the navigation lights either side of the tail fairing. The tailcone is finished in the same grey-green colour as the missile warning antenna fairing.

DANGER
JET BLAST

View of the fin surfaces of a IV(AC) Sqn Harrier GR.7, clearly showing the position of the formation light strips. The small stainless-steel coloured device on the fin surfaces is a temperature probe, while the 'bump' on the fin top houses the radar beacon antenna.

BELOW: Close-up of the special tail markings applied to one of the Harrier GR.7s of 20(R) Sqn during 2001. Note the revised position of the fin flash.

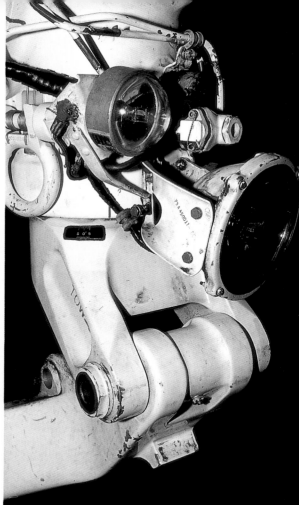

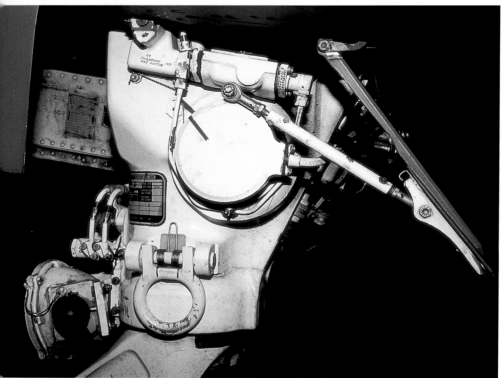

TOP LEFT: General view of the nose undercarriage leg and wheel. The leg is finished in gloss white with black fittings. Note the red service markings and the spring-mounted tie-down ring.

TOP RIGHT: Upper section of the Dowty levered-suspension nose undercarriage leg. Note the position of the landing/taxiing lamps, the spring-mounted tie-down ring and the large amount of piping and cabling that adorns the leg.

BOTTOM: Side view of the upper section of the nose undercarriage leg, which provides some useful references on the style of the small door that sits just behind the leg. Note the position of the door and the hydraulic jacks that control its movement.

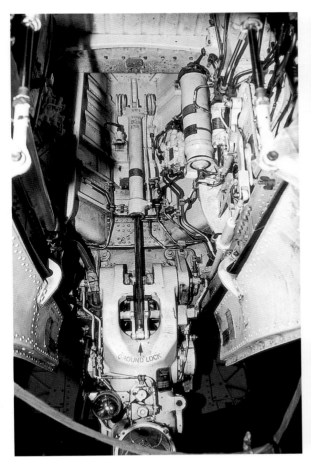 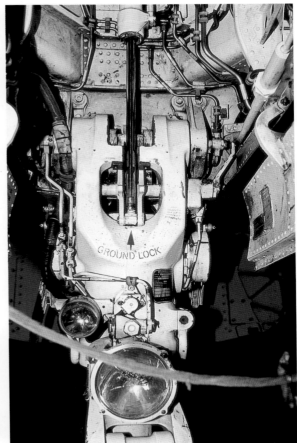

TOP: Two views of the internal structure of the nose undercarriage bay provide a wealth of photographic detail for the advanced modeller. Note the shape of the upper section of the undercarriage leg. The bay is primarily gloss white in colour, with black or stainless steel piping or hosing. Note also the extensive use of yellow connection clips.

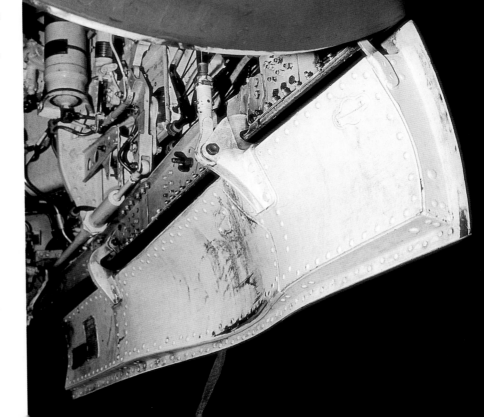

BOTTOM: The gloss white internal structure of one of the primary nose undercarriage doors. The distinctive shape of the door and the location of the hinges are particularly noteworthy.

Two views, port and starboard, of the main undercarriage wheels. The main undercarriage leg is normally gloss white in colour, which quickly deteriorates in service to a semi-gloss sheen. The main wheels' hubs can have either a white or natural metal finish although this quickly becomes gunmetal-coloured in service. Note that, as with all Harrier variants, the main undercarriage bay doors are normally closed when the aircraft is at rest on the ground.

View of the starboard outrigger strut and wheel. The main strut and most of the outrigger assembly are gloss white. Note the tie-down ring.

INSERT: Close-up photograph of one of the outrigger wheels. Note the style and position of the scissors-style actuators.

Port outrigger assembly. The hydraulic retraction jack has a considerable amount of black or grey cabling and piping. Note also the scissors assembly.

Two views showing the internal structure of the outrigger fairing and housing. Note the triangular shape and style of the outrigger doors and the position of the locking arms in the fairing. Internal finish is gloss white throughout.

BELOW: Close-up shot of the Smiths Industries dual combiner pilots Head-Up Display (HUD), which can display FLIR imagery.

TOP LEFT: Close-up of the top section of the pilot's control column, which has a semi-gloss black finish.

TOP RIGHT: Close up of the left-hand cockpit framing, which reveals a plethora of switches and fittings, and a stopwatch. The two small black boxes in the foreground are mounted on the canopy framing and house low-intensity lights for use with night vision goggles. The yellow-coloured surround to these boxes is, in fact, where the black paint has been worn away through use.

BOTTOM: General view of the left-hand side of the cockpit, dominated by two large multifunction display screens either side of the central panel, which houses more conventional instruments. The cockpit area is predominantly mid-grey in colour, in contrast with black or dark grey instruments or panels. The blue of the multifunction display screen and the location of the control column are noteworthy. The small black boxes mounted on the canopy framing and on the right-hand cockpit sidewall, above the radio controls, house low-intensity lights for use with night vision goggles.

TOP: Two further views of the left-hand side of the cockpit. This area of the instrument panel contains the weapon control panel, below the multifunction display screen. The red weapons jettison button and the emergency switches are all outlined in yellow- and black-striped squares. The left-hand side console houses switches for the environmental control system, undercarriage and flying control surfaces.

BOTTOM LEFT: The cockpit area behind the left-hand side of the MB ejection seat is predominantly semi-gloss black in colour.

OPPOSITE PAGE:

TOP: General view showing the lower section of the Martin-Baker Mk 12 ejection seat and demonstrating the level of wear and tear to which these cockpits have been subjected during almost 15 years of operational service.

BOTTOM: The right-hand side console area houses more controls, including those for the environmental control system and some of the self-defence systems, including IFF. Note also the bronze-coloured ejection seat straps.

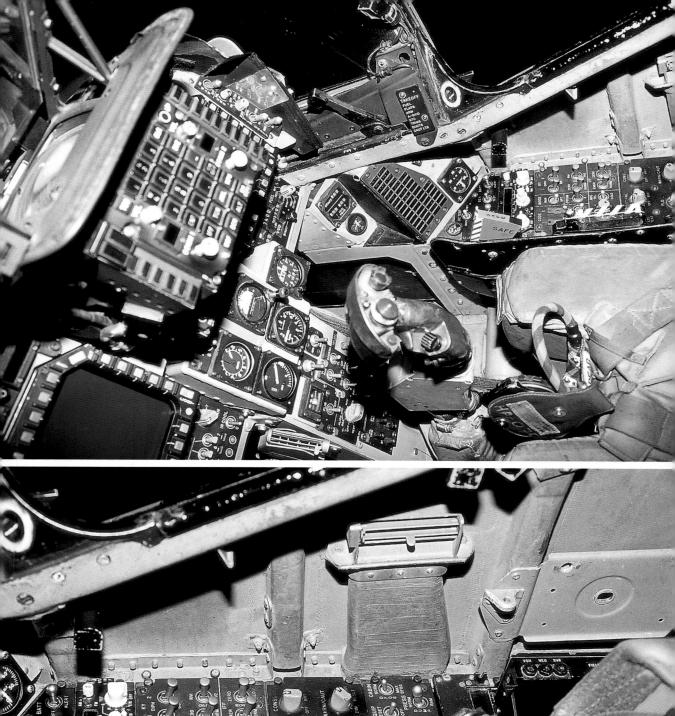

TOP RIGHT: The upper section of the MB Mk 12 ejection seat, part of the cockpit canopy and the rear cockpit bulkhead. The ejection seat top box is semi-gloss black in colour, which contrasts well with the bronze-coloured harness straps

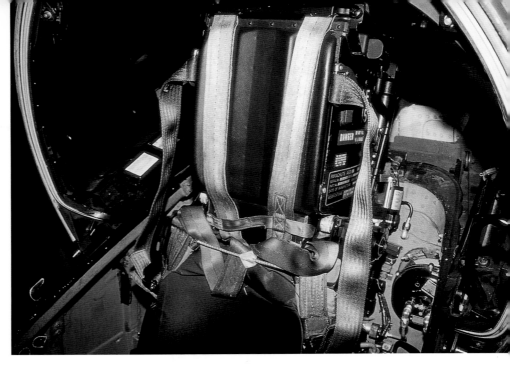

The upper section of the MB Mk 12 seat, which shows the position of the upper safety harness and provides some useful detail on the fittings and fixtures that appear on the rear surfaces of the main seat assembly. Note also the seat manufacturer's data panel and the red warning notices on the side surfaces of the seat top box.

The lower section of the MB Mk 12 ejection seat, graphically illustrating the style and colour of the seat cushion. Note the location of the main ejection seat handle, traditionally outlined in black and yellow, and the main turnbuckle for the seat harness.

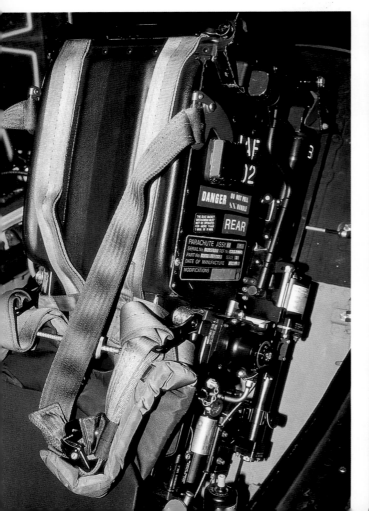

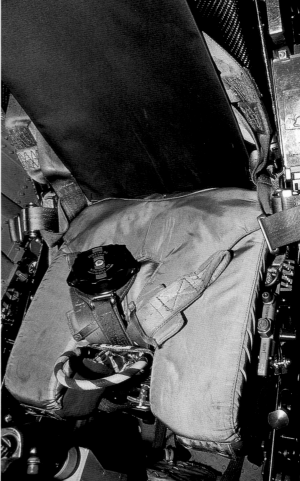

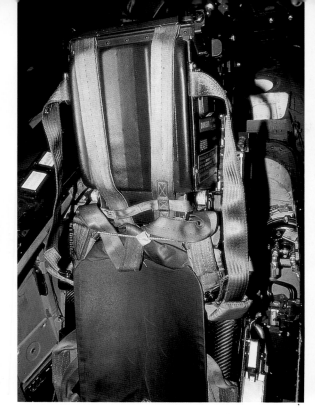
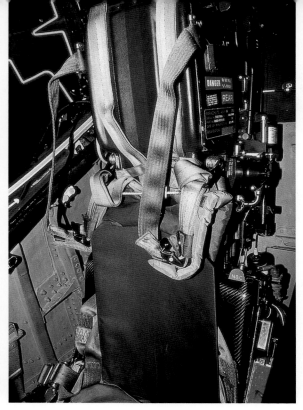

General view of the middle *(left)* and top section *(right)* of the MB Mk 12 ejection seat, which provides some more detail on the shape and colour of the seat backpad. The light blue 'NBC' sign refers to the fitting used with the AR5 NBC set, which is now rarely used or exercised. The red 'rear' notice indicates that this is the rear ejection seat in a T.10 operational trainer.

BELOW: Another view of the lower part of the MB Mk 12 ejection seat, showing the predominance of bronze-coloured safety harnesses and the grey-green seat cushion.

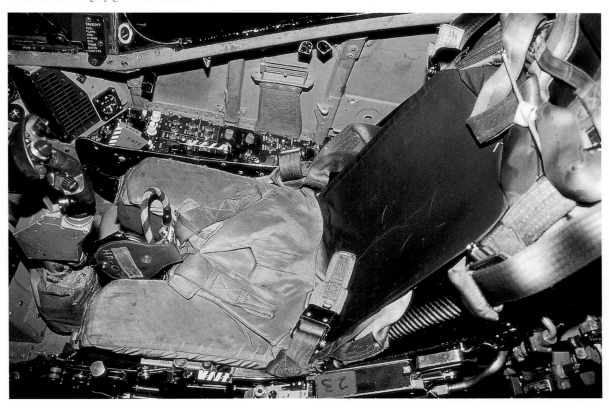

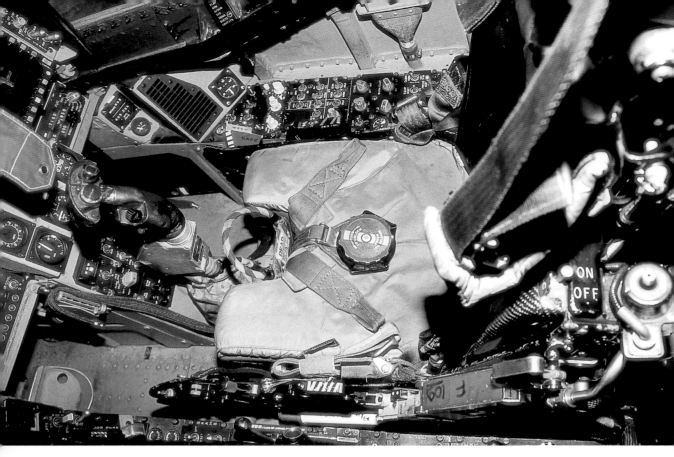

The rear cockpit area of the T.10 operational trainer. Note the dark blue leg restraint cords draped over the central pillar of the main instrument panel.

BELOW: The right-hand side console in the rear cockpit of the T.10 differs slightly from that found in the front of the single-seat GR.7 variant.

External view of the rear screen and canopy on the two-seat T.10 variant of the Harrier. The cockpit consoles are semi-gloss black in colour. Note the piping running along the side of the rear seat console and the Minature Detonating Cord (MDC) pattern in the cockpit canopies.

BELOW: This view, taken from the right-hand side of the aircraft, shows the front cockpit canopy of the T.10, in the open position. Unlike the single-seat GR.7, where the cockpit canopy slides backwards, those on the trainer version are hinged to the right. This view shows the MDC pattern on the front canopy and also reveals that this aircraft is allocated to the Squadron Commander of the OCU, 20(R) Sqn.

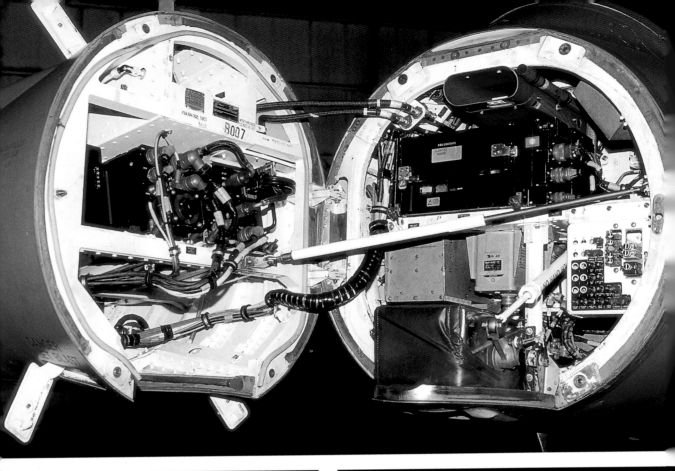

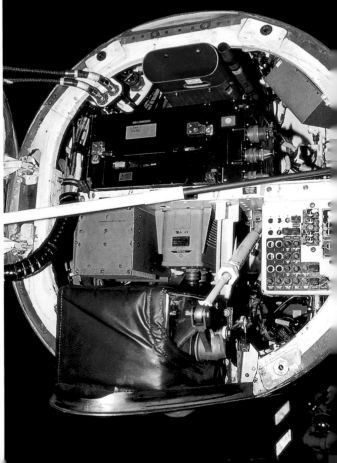

TOP: The nose of the Harrier GR.7 hinges outwards to allow technicians easy access to the avionics suite for the laser target seeker/tracker and FLIR installation. The avionics bay is predominately white, housing an array of black and dark grey Line Replacement Units (LRUs). Note the actuating arm and the black tubing for cable runs.

BOTTOM LEFT: Close-up of the forward section of the hinged nose showing the rear section of one of the LRUs and providing a wealth of detail on the layout of the cabling.

BOTTOM RIGHT: The forward fuselage bulkhead, with a host of detail relating to the avionics installation. Note the brown-coloured fairing and pipe at the top, which forms part of the cooling system for the avionics bays.

THIS PAGE:

TOP: This large access panel is located under the forward fuselage. Note the yellow-green primer finish on the internal surfaces.

BOTTOM: The open access panel on the forward fuselage, which reveals some of the flying control units and part of the ducting for the aircraft's cooling system.

The open access panels on the lower surfaces of the engine air intake, adjacent to the leading edge of the lateral fuselage strake.

BELOW: A technician attends to the topping up of a hydraulic reservoir, providing some useful reference material for model diorama builders.

This overhead view of the outer mainplane shows the position of the vortex generators, including one that has clearly been repaired 'in the field'. It also reveals how quickly the grey camouflage can deteriorate and the colour of the protective material used on the wing leading edges. Note also the position of the RWR antenna and navigation light in the wing-tip.

BELOW: Close-up of the open access panel on the upper surfaces of the port mainplane, which houses the aileron hydraulic actuator.

View of the inner structure of the Harrier GR.7 lower wing root, showing the construction of the ribs and the forward mounting bracket for the mainplane. In keeping with most of the internal structure, the surface finish is yellow-green primer in colour. Note also the two open hatches; the internal structure of the majority of access bays is gloss white.

Two views of the engine bay, which houses the Rolls-Royce Pegasus 11 Mk 105 engine. The centre is dominated by the alternator; the silver drum at bottom right is the engine oil tank. The internal surfaces of the engine access hatches and the actuators are dirty white in colour, while the forward bulkhead of the engine bay itself appears to be a unique green primer colour, which does not match the rest of the airframe. Note also the position of the heat exchanger ram air intakes, forward of the engine bay and adjacent to the cockpit canopy.

OPPOSITE PAGE:
TOP: Another view of the engine bay, showing the rear section that houses the gas turbine starter/auxiliary power unit and its silver exhaust outlet.

BOTTOM: This view shows the shape of the rear access door for the engine bay and provides some useful detail on the internal ribbing construction of this particular panel.

THIS PAGE:
INSET: The hydraulic bay cover in the open position. This whole area of the airframe, which also houses the main refuelling point for the aircraft, has a scruffy appearance.

Another hydraulic bay access door is located mid-way along the starboard side of the fuselage.

The external ground power unit socket on the lower edge of the port fuselage, mid-way between the leading edge of the mainplane and the all-moving tailplane.

BELOW: Unusual view of the rudder hydraulic actuator, with the access cover removed for servicing. This actuator is located at the base of the leading edge of the fin surfaces.

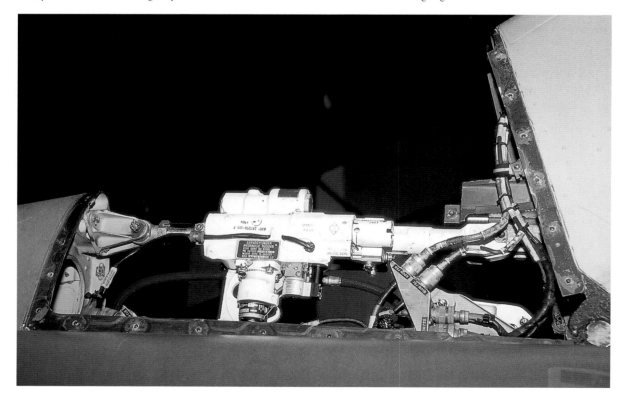

TOP: The tail-mounted yaw and pitch control reaction valves and nozzles, with their access cover removed for routine servicing. Note the sooty appearance of the bay.

BOTTOM: The port outer wing stores pylon.

The port inner wing stores pylon, with Carrier Bomb Light Stores (CBLS) attached. The red warning triangles on the outer surfaces of the pylon and CBLS are also applied to the inner surfaces of the two components. These markings warn personnel of the presence of the explosive charges used to assist with the jettison of stores in flight.

BELOW: Close-up of the stores sway braces used to mount the CBLS to the stores pylon.

Left- and right-hand views of the forward section of the BOL 300 chaff dispenser and AIM-9L acquisition round. The BOL 300 dispenser, developed by Sweden's CelsiusTech, has been designed to be fitted to standard missile launch rails, such as the US LAU-7 or British CRL system. The integrated pod replaces dedicated chaff pods, such as Phimat, previously carried by the Harrier GR.7, and frees up valuable hardpoints for stores carriage. Each BOL 300 launcher can carry 160 chaff packages.

Another view of the BOL 300 chaff dispenser/missile launch rail, fitted to the starboard wing pylon.

BELOW: General view showing one of the standard weapons/stores fits on the port pylon group, including a drop tank, Sidewinder acquisition round and CBLS.

Starboard side view showing a drop tank fitted to the main stores pylon and the BOL 300 chaff dispenser/missile launch rail. This view also provides some useful reference on the blade-shaped fairing adjacent to the lower surfaces of the engine air intake and the outrigger undercarriage assembly.

BELOW: Close-up view of the stores braces linking the drop tank to the main stores pylon on the Harrier GR.7.

Inner surfaces of the starboard outer wing stores pylon.

BELOW: A 'clean' starboard main stores pylon, providing a clear view of the stores sway brace arrangement on this large pylon. Note also the position of the red warning triangle and the anti-abrasion strip on the leading edge of the pylon.

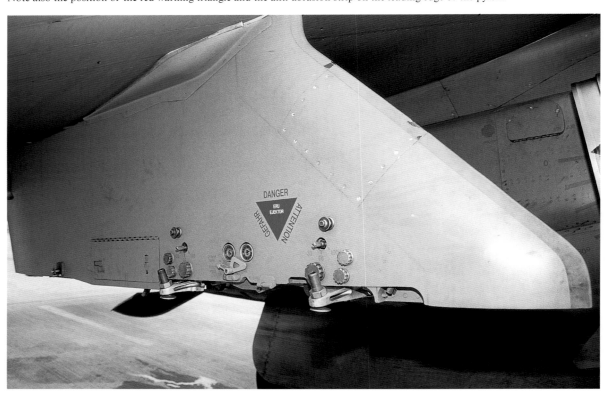

A Harrier GR.7 fitted with a dummy general-purpose 1,000lb bomb, fitted with a No 117 retarding tail unit and a white CRV-7 rocket pod. The modern CRV-7 weapons system, developed in Canada, was successfully used in 1991 by the RAF Jaguar force during Operation *Granby*, the UK contribution to Operation *Desert Storm*. CRV-7 has since been adopted by both the RAF Jaguar and Harrier force as the natural successor to the French-built 68mm Matra 155 'SNEB' pod.

Close-up view of the BOL 300 chaff dispenser and AIM-9L acquisition round.

Harrier T.4

OPPOSITE PAGE:

TOP: This superbly restored BAe Harrier T.4, wearing 20(R) Sqn markings, resides in one of the squadron hangars at RAF Wittering. The airframe is virtually complete, apart from its Rolls-Royce Pegasus 11 Mk 103 engine and a large part of the cockpit area, including the MB Mark 9 zero-zero ejection seats.

BOTTOM: This close-up view of the 'dolphin' nose, which was fitted to both the single-seat GR.3 and the two-seat T.4, provides a useful comparison with the nose shape of the second-generation Harrier II family. This nose housed the Laser Ranging and Marked Target Seeking system (LRMTS), integrated with the Ferranti 541 inertial navigation-attack system, providing the first-generation Harrier with a quantum leap in ground attack and close air support capability.

THIS PAGE:

Two views of the forward (cold) jet exhaust nozzle on the T.4, which, when compared with the more sophisticated nozzles found on the second-generation Harrier family, show just how much progress has been made with the basic design. Note the datum point markers, in black, applied to the fuselage sides – a distinctive feature on all members of the early-generation Harrier and Sea Harrier family. The very thin ventral fuselage strakes (seen at the bottom of the photograph) provided a modicum of improved aerodynamic handling when the Aden gun pods were not fitted.

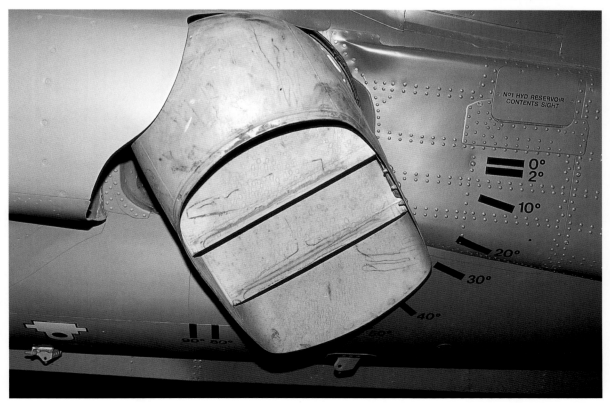

The mainplane of the T.4 was significantly different from that found on the Harrier II aircraft. Note in particular the position of the wing vortex generators and the position of the outrigger fairing and the upper vent for the roll control reaction air valve. The position and shape of the navigation light, wing fences and fuel dump pipe, located on the leading edge between the primary flying control surfaces, are also noteworthy.

BELOW: Close-up view of the port wing-tip, showing the position of the outrigger, which appears to be of a more robust design than that found on the Harrier II aircraft.

View showing the main undercarriage and door. (The main undercarriage doors on all Harrier variants are not normally deployed when the aircraft is parked, unless there is specific maintenance required.) Note the markings on the outer surfaces of the door, which alert groundcrew to the proximity of replenishment bays for the nitrogen and water systems.

BELOW: Close-up of the main wheel and undercarriage leg. Note the position of the small auxiliary undercarriage door, linked to the leg.

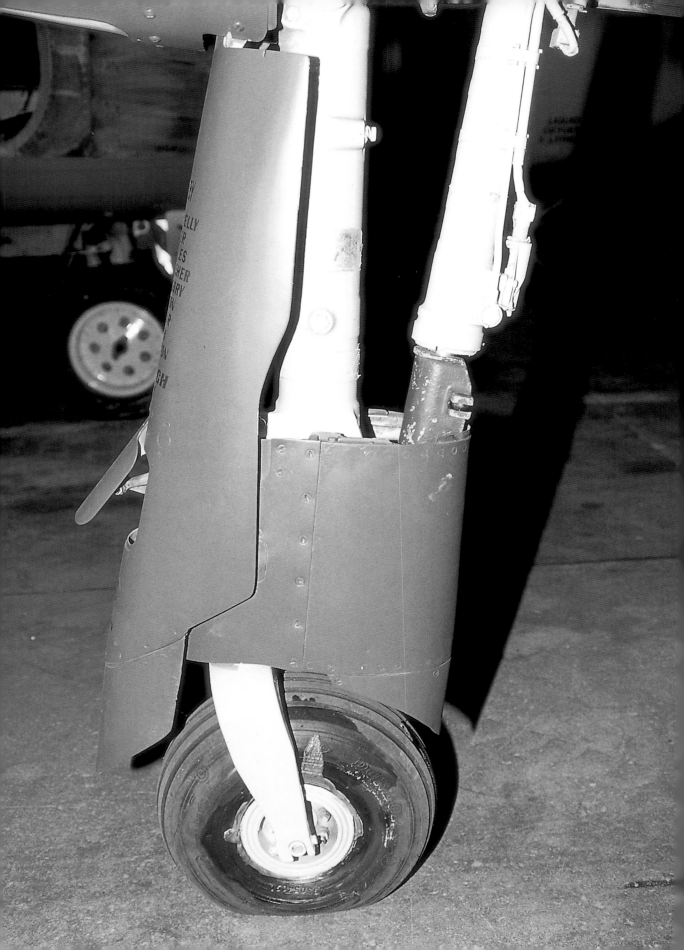

OPPOSITE PAGE: Close-up showing the more robust construction of the port outrigger. Unlike the second-generation Harrier II, more of the aerodynamic section of the outer wing was attached to the outrigger leg. Note the red-painted bracket, a safety fitting, which would be removed before flight.

ABOVE: The fuselage heat shield, adjacent to the rear (hot) jet exhaust nozzle, provides an interesting comparison with that fitted to the Harrier II.

BELOW: The ventral air brake in the deployed position. The outer edges of the air brake protruded on retraction, providing two miniature aerodynamic ventral strakes.

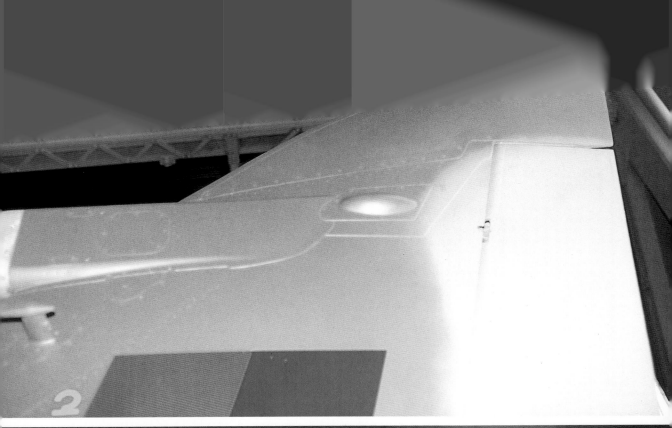

OPPOSITE PAGE:

TOP: General view of the rear of the T.4 fuselage, showing the uncomplicated design of the all-moving tailplane, which is largely unchanged on the second-generation Harrier II.

BOTTOM: Fin surfaces of the preserved 20(R) Sqn Harrier T.4. The large badge is of non-standard design and was never carried by the Harrier T.4 when in operational squadron service.

THIS PAGE:

TOP: Close-up of the upper section of the fin surfaces, which clearly shows the position of the Radar Warning Receiver (RWR) in the leading edge fairing, with its tan-coloured cap, and the temperature probe located on the fin surfaces just below. Note also the standard yellow jacking symbol next to the upper part of the RAF fin flash.

BOTTOM: The large rear boom of the Harrier T.4, which was designed to compensate for the additional weight, and subsequent alteration in the trim and distribution of the heavier two-seat trainer. This boom housed the rear pitch and yaw reaction control ducts and nozzles and the rear-facing RWR antenna. Note the large white rectangular warning notice adjacent to one of the sideways-facing control ducts.

Sea Harrier FRS.1

Sea Harrier FRS.1 ZD610/312 of 899 Naval Air Squadron on the flight line at RAF Yeovilton. The aircraft is in an overall dark grey colour scheme, with toned-down squadron markings, which were adopted across the Sea Harrier fleet after the Falklands War. The radome has been opened to allow maintenance access to the Blue Fox airborne intercept radar. The radome, along with the pitot probe, hinges to port to allow the Sea Harrier to use the lifts on the *Invincible* Class aircraft carriers.

BELOW: Head-on view of a Sea Harrier FRS.1, which shows the angle of the bolt-on inflight-refuelling probe and the demarcation line between the camouflage scheme and the inner gloss-white surfaces of the air intakes.

Two views looking forward along the wing leading edge, showing the position of the inflight-refuelling probe and the auxiliary intake doors. The effects of gravity are clear on the doors and there is a freshly painted panel on the fairing covering the forward jet exhaust nozzle. Note the position of the vortex generators and the wing fences along the leading edge of the wing in the second photograph.

Close-up of the nose of a Sea Harrier FRS.1, clearly showing the position of the pitot probe, above the Blue Fox radar installation, and the inflight-refuelling probe. The Sea Harrier FRS.1 was equipped with the Ferranti Blue Fox multi-mode radar, which had originally been developed from the Seaspray search radar used in early versions of the Royal Navy Lynx helicopter, with new air-to-air modes fitted.

BELOW: Close-up view along the upper surfaces of the Sea Harrier FRS.1 mainplane. Note the position of the upper vent for the roll control reaction air valve, and the scruffy condition of the paintwork.

Close-up of the port outer stores pylon with a missile launch rail and AIM-9 Sidewinder acquisition round mounted. There is a plethora of markings on these components and on the outer surfaces of the drop tank, fitted to the inner pylon.

BELOW: General view of a two-seat Harrier T.4N of 899 Naval Air Squadron in the recently adopted overall gloss-black colour scheme, applied to all UK training aircraft. The two-seat trainer is not equipped with the Blue Fox radar although some special-to-type instruments were fitted, distinguishing the aircraft from the standard T.4, before the latter was withdrawn from RAF service. The 30mm Aden gun pods have obviously been 'robbed' from a frontline single-seat Sea Harrier.

Sea Harrier F/A-2

Rear three-quarter shot of Sea Harrier F/A-2 ZH803/128/R of 800 Naval Air Squadron, sporting a full offensive load, with no less than four AIM-9L Sidewinder missiles on the outer wing pylons and a pair of AIM-120 AMRAAMs on fuselage-mounted 'shoulder' pylons. The 'R' designation on the fin signifies the squadron's assignment to the HMS *Ark Royal* Carrier Air Group.

BELOW: View of the starboard forward fuselage clearly showing the position of the auxiliary intake doors, when the aircraft is at rest and the open position of the cockpit canopy. Note also the position of the national and low-visibility safety/warning markings and the RBF tags.

ABOVE: Sea Harrier F/A-2
XZ459/126/R of 800 NAS,
which is presented in the ground
attack/close air support role, armed
with two 1,000lb GP bombs and
a pair of 30mm Aden gun pods.
The full colour red Unit markings
made a welcome return in 1999,
following their removal in the days
leading up to the squadron's
deployment as part of the
Falkland Islands Task Force
in April 1982.

Close-up of XZ459's centre
section, showing the outrigger
wheel and bomb to advantage.

Two close-up views of the most obvious change between the shape of the FRS.1 and the F/A-2 airframe. The rounder, shorter nose radome houses the more advanced Ferranti Blue Vixen radar, developed after the experiences of the Sea Harrier force during the Falklands War. The Blue Vixen radar gives genuine all-weather lookdown/shootdown capability, with improved range and multiple target tracking capability, making it one of the most capable radar systems in the world today.

Close-up of the cockpit canopy on the Sea Harrier F/A-2. Note the location of the air inlets on the upper decking of the air intakes and the type and style of markings found around the canopy area.

BELOW: Close-up of the lower portion of the starboard forward fuselage below the cockpit, showing the position of the various air scoops and antenna that occupy this area. The aperture for the F95 camera is also visible.

Close-up of the auxiliary engine intake doors and air intake on a very clean-looking Sea Harrier F/A-2.

BELOW: Close-up shot of the forward exhaust nozzle, fairing and dump pipe. Note the positional indicators, this time in white, around the forward exhaust nozzle.

Close-up of the white datum markings adjacent to the forward exhaust nozzle and the blade-shaped fairing, both of which appear common to all first- and second-generation Harrier variants.

BELOW: General view of the 30mm Aden gun pod fitted to the starboard lower fuselage surfaces. This pod is identical to that fitted to the earlier RAF Harrier GR.1 and GR.3 variants as well as the Sea Harrier FRS.1.

Fin surfaces of a Sea Harrier F/A-2 of 800 NAS clearly showing the position of the re-located pitot probe and the RWR fairing in the leading edge of the fin. Note the angle of the all-moving taileron when the aircraft is at rest.

BELOW: View of the lower rear fuselage, showing the various vents and antenna in this area of the aircraft.

Two views of the twin AIM-9L Sidewinder missile installation on the Sea Harrier F/A-2. There are various colours featured on the AIM-9L, and a vast number of safety and warning markings.

BELOW: Head-on shot of the twin AIM-9L Sidewinder fit on the starboard weapons pylon.

TOP: Close-up view of the seeker heads of the AIM-9L Sidewinder.

BOTTOM: General view of a 1,000lb GP bomb fitted to the starboard outer pylon of the Sea Harrier F/A-2. This is a standard weapon, used by both the RAF and FAA Harrier force.

Two views of the AIM-120 AMRAAM and the 'shoulder'-mounted fuselage pylon fitted to the starboard side of a Sea Harrier F/A-2. This missile, now combined with the highly effective Blue Vixen radar, gives the F/A-2 a formidable operational capability in its primary role of air defence.

Harriers At Large

An early development Harrier GR.5A conducting weapons load trials with a pair of AIM-9 Sidewinders, two Paveway II LGBs and a Phimat chaff dispenser on the port outer stores pylon; the latter was used before the delivery of the BOL 300 chaff dispensing system. (Photo: copyright BAe Systems plc)

BELOW: Harrier GR.7 ZD407/36 of 233 OCU/20(R) Sqn launches a salvo from its CRV-7 rocket pods over a weapons range in northern England. The aircraft wears the current two-tone grey camouflage scheme. (Photo: copyright Geoffrey H. Lee/BAe Systems plc)

A two-seat T.10 operational trainer (ZH658/N) of 20(R) Sqn. Note the ventral fuselage strakes fitted for this particular sortie. (Photo: copyright BAe Systems plc)

BELOW: Sea Harrier FRS.1 of 899 NAS about to launch from the deck of an *Invincible* Class aircraft carrier of the Royal Navy. Note the position of the air brake and the all-moving taileron in this view. (Photo: copyright BAe Systems plc)

THIS PAGE: A pair of 899 NAS Sea Harrier FRS.1s low over countryside near their home base of RNAS Yeovilton in Somerset. The two aircraft wear the overall dark grey camouflage scheme adopted after the Falklands War and are carrying two different weapons fits. The nearest aircraft (711) is carrying a AIM-9 Sidewinder acquisition round while '715' carries the twin AIM-9 Sidewinder pylons with live rounds fitted. (Photo: copyright BAe Systems plc)

OPPOSITE PAGE:

TOP: A superb photograph showing a wealth of detail on one of the standard weapons fits for the Sea Harrier FRS.1. Apart from a pair of drop tanks, which are almost standard fit on the Sea Harrier, this aircraft also carries a pair of 30mm Aden gun pods and two pairs of AIM-9 Sidewinders on their twin rails. This photograph also provides invaluable reference on the amount of staining that can appear on the lower fuselage surfaces of the Sea Harrier in service. (Photo: copyright BAe Systems plc)

BOTTOM: A similar photograph of a Sea Harrier F/A-2 provides more valuable reference on the noticeable effect of the rear jet exhaust nozzle on the rear fuselage, which is even more pronounced on this particular airframe. The light grey colour scheme is very susceptible to all manner of wear and tear during operational service. (Photo: copyright BAe Systems plc)

Air-to-air shot of an unmarked Sea Harrier F/A-2 high above its home base at RNAS Yeovilton in Somerset. The aircraft carries a pair of 30mm Aden gun pods and AIM-9L Sidewinder missiles. (Photo: copyright BAe Systems plc)

USMC McDonnell Douglas AV-8B Harrier II Plus 165001/YM-54 taxies out of its revetment during the Royal International Air Tattoo, RAF Fairford, 1999. The radar-equipped Harrier II Plus can be distinguished from its earlier cousin, the AV-8B, by the re-contoured nose, which houses the Hughes AN/APG-65 pulse-Doppler radar.

BELOW: McDonnell Douglas AV-8A(S) Matador 01-804/4 of Escaudrilla 008 arrives at RAF Fairford for the International Air Tattoo in July 1994.

The McDonnell Douglas TAV-8s of Escaudrilla 008, based at Cadiz/Rota, were very rarely seen outside Spain so the appearance of this specially marked two-seater (c/n 01-808/8) at RAF Fairford for the International Air Tattoo in July 1994 was a real treat for aviation enthusiasts. Note the unit badge, carried on the nose of all Escaudrilla 008 AV-8 Matadors.

BELOW: In 1987 the Spanish Arma Aerea de la Armada reequipped with the McDonnell Douglas/BAE AV-8B Harrier II, which equipped Escaudrilla 009 at Rota AB. In Spanish Armada service the aircraft carry the designation EAV-8B but do not carry individual serial numbers. This particular aircraft, coded 01-905, was one of the first batch of AV-8Bs procured by Spain and was photographed at RNAS Yeovilton in 1994. Spain has since received a second batch of the more capable radar-equipped AV-8B Harrier II Plus aircraft, which are also operated by Escaudrilla 009 at Rota. The remaining EAV-8Bs are being reworked to the same standard.